What My ~~influence in my life.~~
Parents
Did Right

A Parenting Guide
From the Perspective of Childhood Memories

Joy Adams

Numbers 6: 24-26

Joy Adams

Dedicated to my mom and dad:

Thank you for all you have done and all that you continue to do in my life. I love you so much, and I pray that this book will honor and bless you

Table of Contents

Acknowledgements

Thank you to my husband, Bruce. You are my best friend, my partner and my forever love. Thank you for supporting me and my dream of becoming a writer. Words could never express my deep love for you. I cherish the journey that we are on, as we day by day, grow old together.

Thank you to my children--Amy, Alexander, Evelyn, Jeremiah and Daniel. I am who I am today because of you. May my ceiling, be your floor.

Thank you to my parents--Bud and Laura Mailhot-- and my sisters--Lacie and Glory--for creating a childhood for me that was filled with love.

Thank you to Tony Sciarini for your encouragement and for editing my manuscript. Your friendship to both Bruce and I is priceless.

Thank you to Bernice Hammond, Shell Cowper- Smith, Pastors Richard and Anna Salmeron, Anna Alveraz, and Shanna Gil. Thank you for taking a chance on me. Thank you for giving your time and energy to read my manuscript and provide insight, support and encouragement.

Thank you to my many friends who have encouraged me, cheered me on, and helped to make me the person I am today. Thank you to Natalie Casey, Katie Fagan, Paramjeet and Gurwinder Gill, Sarah Griffith, Pastors Tom and Bernice Hammond, Debora Roadruck, Raquel Sanchez, Vanessa Coporan, Pastors Scott and Melissa Sherwood, and Pastors Jose and Shanna Gil.

Thank you to Pastors Ron and Jennifer Eivaz and all of our Harvest Church, Turlock, family. The thirteen years that we got to be a part of your church family was priceless. All of our family's core values were birthed from the Harvest Church culture. It was actually a Harvest Life Group, led by Sheila Taylor that inspired me to start writing this book.

Thank you to our Luz De Valle, Hayward, church family. Our cultures, language and customs may be different, but we have found our home with you. Thank you for accepting our family and for helping us to give our children a portal into the nations.

Joy Adams has done an exceptional job providing inspiration and tools to strengthen every family. The concept alone of writing positive things one has learned from their parents is genius, but Joy Adams goes far beyond as she delivers pithy, practical truths with such clarity. She brings the stories to life so that they stick with you and leaves you with a way to apply the insights right away. This book is valuable to families of all ages and stages, and can even help the empty nesters among us who desire to strengthen all our relationships.

Shell Cowper-Smith; Family Coach, Youth Advocate, Foster parent since 1984

I loved *What My Parents Did Right*! I've never read a parenting book that was written from a personal experience like this one. I wish I had my hands on it years ago. There are several things from this book, I will take and implement with my kids. What I love most is that I know Joy Adams and her character--She is living proof that the truths in this book really work.

I had the pleasure of working with Joy Adams in youth ministry for several years and was able to see the fruit of the truths her parents planted in her life coming to fruition in her life. I also saw this fruit in the way she related to and taught our students and now in the way she pours into her own children

What My Parents Did Right is filled with principles and foundational truths that unfortunately most parents do not think to teach until there is an issue. The questions that she has at the end of the chapters along with the scripture verses, give parents the opportunity to reflect and make any adjustments based on what we may have learned. I love that this book is not Joy giving advice, but giving truths that actually worked, and she is a living example.

What My Parents Did Right is a must read for all parents!

Shanna Gil, mother of five

Reading this book, *What My Parents Did Right* by author Joy Adams was like taking a breath of fresh air. What a testimony to share! The idea that as parents, you can leave a legacy for your children, even if your own parents fell short, is truly inspiring.

This book is not only a delight to read but it is also very informative especially for young couples raising their children, looking and seeking for ways to help guide them in a Godly way. This book would also be an awesome resource to share in small groups. As pastors for over 20 years we have had the opportunity to counsel many families throughout the years. The majority of people carry so much anguish and resentment from the past towards their parents. This book can be used to inspire parents to create a fresh path for their family and build a legacy.

You can be a game changer and be the parent you wanted for yourself.

Richard and Anna Salmeron
Senior Pastors, Luz del Valle church,
Hayward, California

What My Parents Did Right is an excellent resource to assist Christian parents in developing the skills needed to raise their children with values that align with the word of God. Author Joy Adams offers her beautiful testimony as an example to help guide families who may not have had the privilege in having a model to learn from. As a Marriage Family Therapist I have seen the struggles families have when they are unsure how to navigate issues related to culture, discipline, conflict, and finances. This guide is a valuable study for parents, small groups, or even a curriculum to use to teach from. Those who apply the tools will feel empowered to parent.

Anna Alvarez, Licensed Marriage Family Therapist
with Cairo Counseling since 2008

From the first moment that we see our growing baby, on an ultrasound screen or when we hold him or her for the very first time, something inside us realizes that suddenly our priorities have changed. All of our other aspirations in life become less significant as we now realize that this precious child will be looking to us for pure and undivided love, care and guidance.

Unlike many other milestones in life – completing school, landing that dream job, buying a house – creating a baby does not require hours of study or a long application and interview process. All that is required is one egg, one sperm, and a relatively healthy and safe place in the mother's womb. For most of us, this rather simple process creates a brand new human being, and that is what we call the miracle of life; no applications or background checks required.

Parents have the mountainous task of being the best parents they can be, and the role of parent is the toughest and most challenging role a person will ever have. Creating that loving and safe environment, fostering healthy growth, providing structure: the list of things "good" parents do in our minds is never ending. This powerful and amazing role of being a parent is granted to us without reservation from the Almighty God, who lovingly and full of grace and mercy allows the honor of parenthood, despite the reality that many of us at one time or another feel unprepared or ill-equipped.

In life, it is easy to go from the moments of euphoria in the delivery room, where there is nothing you would not do for your child, to the day-to-day, where the best of intentions fall into compromise. The same parent who swore that she would never use the TV as free childcare now regularly sends the kids out of the kitchen, suggesting they watch a show while mommy makes dinner. It is easy to slip from a stance of "I am never going to do (fill-in the bank), like my parents did," to an "I lived through it and so can they" attitude. This leads to the question: Do you want your kids to survive or do you want them to thrive?

Often as parents, we forget that as we are rushing about our day, we constantly have an audience. Our children are forming memories that will likely influence them for the rest of their lives, not based on our best intentions, but based on the day-to-day that they experience.

I had the blessing of growing up in a loving, two-parent Christian home. The experiences I had growing up are now fond memories that often serve as my go-to resource when it comes to raising my own children. The memories I share in the following chapters are the lessons I learned from growing up in my parents' home. It is these memories that have influenced my life in multiple ways. My decisions as a child and teenager, my relationship with my husband, my teaching style (I taught high school for nine years and loved it), the way

I serve in ministry, and so much more of what I do stems from the things that my parents did.

My parents were and continue to be great parents (and now excellent grandparents too). I know that it is the memories and experiences that I had growing up that propelled me through adolescence and into adulthood. I believe that my successes are truly a result of great parenting. It is my hope and prayer that by sharing these memories with you, you will find yourself empowered, realizing that you, too--- no matter what your background is--- can be a great parent.

The same job that requires no education, applications or interviews is in fact the most important job we will ever be given. God in His mercy has allowed us the amazing role of parenthood, packed full with life's biggest joys and biggest challenges, and with His help, I pray that you will see that we are *all* up to the task

Chapter 1: Memories

Growing up, it seemed as though my parents used every opportunity available to speak good things into my life and to foster healthy, loving relationships. Moments shared together doing chores or while en route to my next piano lesson have become priceless memories that have served as a navigational system for my life.

Once, while in the car with my mom, my mom and I heard a man on a Christian radio program say that most people's attitudes about life are defined by their first memory. After hearing this program, my mom asked me what my earliest memory was. I thought back and could narrow down my earliest memory to one of two memories. In both memories, I was about two or three years old, and with both memories, I can look back even now with clarity. In one memory, I remember being held by my mom in her rocking chair as she rubbed my back and sang to me. I remember feeling very comfortable, safe, and loved. My other memory is of me going into my parents' bedroom and seeing my mother kneeling by the bed praying. I remember that she had tears in her eyes when she looked up to see me. Usually, to see my mom crying would have caused me to be alarmed, but the smile that she gave me when she looked up told me that she was just fine. Instead of being worried about her tears, I just remember feeling happy to know that my mom had been talking to Jesus.

I do not know if there is any actual truth to the statement the man on the radio made, but I do know that my childhood was filled with great memories, and just like my two earliest memories, most of them involve one or both of my parents. When I was a child, I never really thought about why my parents did the things that they did. However, looking back as an adult, I have come to realize that pretty much everything they did as parents they did not by accident or even by instinct, but with purpose.

Both of my parents came from families that lacked the safe and loving environment that I grew up with. Specifically, they lacked healthy fathers. I remember once as a teenager remarking to my mom that I thought it was weird that the family of one of my friends never hugged. My mom then explained to me that things like that do not always come naturally. She told me that when she was growing up, her family rarely hugged each other or had any kind of healthy physical interactions. In fact, the only time she ever

remembered her dad hugging her was once when she
had asked him to. He answered her by grabbing her
a mocking way and hugged her in a very rough fashio
to the point that it hurt. She never asked him again.
My mom then explained to me that coming from such
home required her to train herself to interact with my
two older sisters and me physically. She explained th
it was difficult at first, but that she had made it a
priority to hug and cuddle us, even though it did not
come naturally. My dad's father was no better. In fa
my paternal grandfather once explained to an ER nur
that he had accidentally hit his younger son in the hea
with a hammer, but he went on to say that he had bee
aiming for his other son, my dad.

Coming from the homes that both my parents came
from, they could have easily continued the cycles they
experienced, and I could have been the result of
generational family dysfunction. It happens so often.
After all, a person can only give what they have and ca
only teach what they know, so that usually this cycle o
dysfunction goes on and on. I am not exactly sure how
my parents broke this cycle. I think that they just
started out as parents deciding in their hearts that the
were going to do things differently than their parents
did. Along the way, they allowed God to give them tool
and strategies through prayer, books, and whatever
else to end the cycle of dysfunction and create an
atmosphere of love and security.

What My Parents Did Right

Throughout the chapters of this book, you will find stories that will spotlight one of my parents rather than both of them. I feel that it is important to say that even though only one of them may be mentioned in a memory, both were equally responsible for the way I was brought up. My parents worked as a team. My dad may have been away from the home working while my mom was homeschooling us or driving us to piano lessons; but the reality is that without my dad working as hard as he did, my mom would not have been able to stay home with my sisters and me. My mom, for example, may have initially been the one to teach a life's lesson during the day, but when my dad came home from work, his life endorsed the lesson by his words and in everything that he did.

I have often heard parents say, "I wonder if my child is even going to remember me doing (<u>fill-in the blank</u>) for them." Well, this is an account of what I do remember, and I know that these memories have not only been foundational in my life, but are also the building blocks of what is now becoming multigenerational family health as I now raise my own children with purpose and intentionality.

Discussion Questions:

1. How have your childhood memories shaped you into the person you are today?
2. How do your childhood experiences affect the way you parent?
3. What memories do you want your child(ren) to grow up with?

"Commit your works to the Lord, and your thoughts will be established."

- Proverbs 16:3

Dear God,

Thank you for being a loving and good Father. Please heal my heart from any wounds from my childhood, and specifically, from the wounds placed there by my earthly parents. Empower me and strengthen me with your love so that I can raise my child(ren) in love. Let my motivations and actions as a parent come from a whole and healthy heart, not a wounded one. Guide me with wisdom as I guide my child(ren) from infancy into adulthood.

Amen.

A ll adults have disagreements from time to time. However, looking back on my years of growing up, I can only remember hearing my parents argue once, and even this argument was not intended to be heard (my parents thought we were sleeping). Whenever my parents had a disagreement (which was not too often), they would always talk it out privately. As we grew older, most often these private conversations would take place in the form of a "drive." My parents would inform us girls that they were going to go for a "drive," and living out in the country as we did, we realized that often a "drive" just meant driving down the dirt road a little ways. Sometimes they would come back twenty minutes later. Other times they would call from town to let us know they had decided to turn their "drive" into a date night and that they would be back in a few hours. Either way, we always knew that when they got back, they would be on the same page, as a team, ready for whatever needed to happen next. When my parents returned from a few of these discussions, I could tell that my mom had been crying, but it was just as obvious that they were a team and that they would continue working as a team.

(As a side note, I think it is important to note that I am the youngest of three girls. My sisters are two and five years older than me, so when my parents went for these "drives," I had adequate supervision. When we were all small, I believe my parents saved their arguments for the basement or out by the barn.)

I also never heard my parents talk about divorce. In fact, they have been married over forty-five years, and it is obvious that only death will separate them.

Throughout their marriage, my parents have had many difficulties in their lives that would have caused many other people to check out on life and/or each other. My dad had various health problems that included lead poisoning, a broken tailbone, and Epstein Barr. Despite these physical setbacks, my dad somehow managed to continue to support the family, always coming home with a smile on his face. My mom also had her hands full with the physical, mental and emotional strain of being a stay-at-home wife and homeschooling mom. The reality is that I think all couples at one point or another have conflict to varying degrees, but I think the key to success that my parents had was that they were very proactive – they did not wait until there was a blowup to start searching for solutions. As we grew up, my parents taught us girls that divorce should never be an option. My parents did not wait until a blowup to go for a "drive." I even remember my parents going to marriage counseling, telling me that even "good" marriages needed some extra work from time to time.

My parents' ability to manage conflict between themselves had, and continues to have, a huge impact on my life. First and foremost, I had the luxury of growing up in a home in which I felt safe. I did not have to walk into a room timidly, wondering if I was coming into a war zone, as too many kids do. I knew that my home was a safe place, and I knew that no matter what challenges life tossed my way, my parents would figure it out. In addition to creating a safe environment, my parents taught us through modeling how to resolve conflict. Yes, my parents did have their "drives," but the reality is that these drives were few and far between. In most cases, my parents were able to talk out their plans and ideas, and when a conflict came up, they were usually able to find a solution. For them, it always seemed to be about the solution. There never seemed to be winners or losers, but just solutions.

Discussion Questions:

1. What is your family norm when it comes to disagreements?

2. What steps can you take to increase healthy communication in your home?
3. When conflict occurs, how is reconciliation achieved?

"A soft answer turns away wrath, but a harsh word stirs up anger."

-   Proverbs 15:1

"Blessed are the peacemakers, for they shall be called sons of God."

-   Mathew 5:9

Dear God,

Help me to be a person of peace. Give me wisdom, compassion and understanding. In times of conflict, remove my competitive spirit that desires to conquer and win. Instead, give me a pure heart that seeks to find the best solutions in the spirit of peace, truth and love. Let my home be a safe place, a place of peace and a place of love. Let my child(ren) learn from my words and actions how to solve conflicts with integrity.

Amen.

Chapter 3: Money Part 1

My dad is and always has been extremely gifted with his hands. Whether it be construction, woodworking, radiators, auto body, you name it and my dad probably has made it or fixed it. These talents, mixed with his entrepreneurial spirit, had him owning several of his own businesses, and with these came the freedom--as well as the struggles--known well to any who have ever owned their own businesses. I would say that for at least half of my childhood, my family did not have health insurance. During Christmas time and tax time, business was usually slower, and so my parents always had to be prepared. My mom bought things in bulk during the busy seasons to prepare for the slower seasons. To us girls, it was normal; but looking back now, I realize that often my mom had to be prepared ahead of time, knowing that there was no guaranteed bi-weekly or monthly check. There were times that I remember my mom sending me into the store to buy a quart of milk. Being from a family of five, I felt this was a very uncommon thing since we always bought milk by the gallon. When I would ask my mom why, she would reply, "Because that is all we need right now." It was not until I was an adult that my mom told me that those "quart-of-milk days" were days in which that was all we could afford.

My parents made sure that their occasional financial limitations did not become our problems. I never remember my parents saying, "We can't afford that" when my sisters and I would ask for something. We did not always get what we were asking for, but the reasons we were given were never that we could not afford it. Instead, they would say something like this:

"Maybe next time."

"I don't think you need that right now."

"Well, I already let you pick out these cookies; if you want the crackers instead, you will have to put back the cookies."

"If that is something you really want, you can do

some extra jobs around the
house and save up for it
yourself."

These replies communicated to us that we would not be getting what we wanted at that exact moment, but it did it in such a way that we were not made to feel like a burden on the family's resources. In fact, some of what they said actually empowered us by allowing us to decide what treat we kept, or by communicating that we had the power and ability to make our own purchases. Instead of being made to feel responsible for our family's financial situation– a situation we as kids had no control over-- we were handed the child-size freedom of choice and personal capability.

Working in youth ministry at my church for over ten years, I have seen time and time again when students will not even try to attend a conference or day trip. Instead, they say, "My family/my parents can't afford it." To me, this is heartbreaking. It is not that I think teenagers should be constantly getting things from their parents. In fact, I do not. It is that they have heard the same answer of "We can't afford it" for so long that they have inherited a poverty mentality from their parents. They do not even realize that they have the power to earn their own way. It does not occur to them that they could do some babysitting or yard work to earn the money. When I am face-to-face with students who have emotionally had to bear the weight of their families' financial problems, it makes me realize how fortunate I was.

When I was a teenager, my parents told me they were no longer going to be in charge of buying my clothes. There would be no more back-to-school shopping, winter/summer shopping trips, etc. Instead, they gave me $35 cash each month, with the exception of December (Christmas) and June (my birthday month). That made for a total of $350 per year that I had to budget myself to purchase my own clothes, including underwear and socks. This was such an empowering financial responsibility. Truly, the money was mine to do with what I wanted. I could save it over the course of several months in order to go on a shopping spree. I could shop for bargains at the local thrift store to see just how far I could stretch my money. I could buy a little each month (at the time, a pair of jeans at Old Navy cost about $22-35, and a shirt ranged from $12-20). I could even blow it all on something non-clothing-related, like going to an amusement park with friends; but if I did that, I would have to be okay with my current wardrobe, and I would have no one to blame but myself if later in the month I was wearing jeans with a tear or a shirt with a stain.

What My Parents Did Right

The responsibility and privilege of being able to make my own choices when it came to my clothing went a long way in developing my budgeting skills, and it empowered me with the freedom of choice. Whether the choice was between premium brand names and inferior brands, or between wash-and-wear and hand wash only, these were choices I got to make; and yes, at this age, my personal laundry was also one-hundred percent my responsibility.

In times of lack and times of abundance, my parents provided a stable, healthy, and age-appropriate view of money, purchases, and choice. I have come to believe that poverty and wealth are really much less about account balances and so much more about choice and empowerment. I suppose that it is fitting that the one Bible verse that my mom made sure that we all knew was "I can do all this through him [Jesus Christ] who gives me strength" (Philippians 4:13, NIV). I fully believe that this verse has implications that exceed its context. However, it was not until I was an adult that I realized that the context of this verse is actually within the topic of poverty and wealth. Combined with the previous verse, the passage reads, "I know what it is to be in need, and I know what it is to have plenty. I have learned to be content in any and every situation, whether well fed or hungry, whether living in plenty or in want. I can do all this through him who gives me strength (Philippians 4:12-13, NIV)."

Discussion Questions:

1. Do you naturally see yourself from a place of wealth or a place of poverty? Is your perception accurate?
2. If you were to ask your child(ren), 'Is our family rich or poor?' how would they respond? Would their perception be accurate?
3. How can you create a culture of prosperity in your home, even if your account balances are lacking?
4. What can you do to instill the power of choice in your child(ren)'s financial mentality?

"I love all who love me.

Those who search will surely find me.

I have riches and honor, as well as enduring wealth and justice.

My gifts are better than gold,

Even the purest gold, my wages better than sterling silver!

I walk in righteousness,

In paths of justice.

Those who love me inherit wealth.

I will fill their treasuries."

\- Proverbs 8:17-21

Dear God,

Train me in my attitudes and behaviors when it comes to finances. Remove any poverty mindsets or behaviors, and replace them with wise decisions, words, and attitudes that come from my place of abundance in You. Let my child(ren) know their identity, true wealth, and value. Let their inheritance be a spirit of abundance, and keep the spirit of poverty far from them.

Amen.

Chapter 4: Money Part 2

When it comes to discussing money, it seems as though many parents are either one extreme or another. Either the parents burden the children with every little aspect of the family's finances--usually all negative--or they keep all discussions of money hidden like a deep, dark secret. Thankfully, my parents seemed to have a very healthy and God-centered understanding of money:

> Everything belongs to God, and it is God who blesses our family with good health and the ability to make money. God is our provider. Therefore, we work to please God and not man. We work hard at our jobs, not out of fear of man, but out of love for God, our provider.

As a child, I remember my dad and mom discussing money. Sometimes, it would be in the form of hearing them budget how they would spend a check that would come in. Other times, it would simply be my dad coming home and letting my mom know that he was leaving a hundred dollar bill on the counter for my mom to buy groceries. Actually, my dad would quite often leave my mom's grocery money on the counter like this, often in the form of a hundred dollar bill. I remember liking to look at it. It was very attractive to me. Sometimes, I would even ask if I could touch it, and my parents always let me, under supervision, of course.

I remember my parents explaining to my sisters and me how interest rates worked. They warned us against credit cards, a lesson that at times in my life I wish I would not have taken for granted. They taught us about financial terms such as "minimum payment," "principal," and "interest." They taught us what common phrases meant, such as "no interest for one year," "rent-to-own," "good credit" and "bad credit." They taught us how to budget by the way they handled their own finances, as well as in the way they helped us manage our own.

My parents always taught that God came first. His *tithe* (tenth) came first out of obedience to Him. We were taught the difference between tithe and offerings, and my parents encouraged us to do both. When we were very young children, my mom would give us coins to drop in the basket as our offering. As we started to acquire money through allowances and chores, my parents taught us how to figure out the tithe, a Sunday school and math lesson all in one. I remember the joy and excitement I felt in being able to place money in the offering plate as it passed by, because I was included as part of the offering process. Even when I was only putting in a quarter or two, I could imagine the church having a need, and my two quarters making the difference. I am so glad that my parents taught us girls to tithe, and also to give offerings. My parents led by example, and I know that it is because they introduced the concept of giving to us when we were young that I never struggled with the obedience aspect of giving. I know that, for many, it is truly a struggle to obey God by giving the tithe. For me, it was easy to be obedient because my parents taught me that giving was an act of joy and that God owned everything anyway. My parents did not teach us these financial lessons all at once, as in a one-time seminar, but they instead sprinkled them in throughout day-to-day life. Whether it was during car rides to church, piano lessons, conversations at the breakfast table, or follow-up conversations after TV shows or movies, our lives were filled with life's lessons, and these lessons included money.

When my sisters and I first began working small jobs as early teens – babysitting, house cleaning, tutoring, and in my case, giving piano lessons, we were taught to tithe first before anything else; then, with the remaining balance, half went into savings, and the other half was for spending money. As we grew older and began driving, my parents taught us a more expanded budget, including gas, car insurance and car maintenance. They taught us that we should expect to pay for new tires, brakes, etc., periodically, but that with proper planning, these expenditures did not need to create havoc in our budget.

Some might think that based on my very sound financial lessons during childhood, my finances are perfectly in order. The reality is that my husband and I do have some debt from time to time, and occasionally, a car or house maintenance expense will sneak up on us before we are fully ready. Real life is not always as predictable as we sometimes want it to be, but with the wise money management skills that we learned growing up my husband and I know how to solve these problems and get back on track.

My parents taught me a lot about finances and good financial planning, but what they impressed on me the most, is that everything belongs to God. Whether it is big or small, stewarding what God gives me with honor and conscientiousness is what it is all about. "I know what it is to be in need, and I know what it is to have plenty. I have learned the secret of being content in any and every situation, whether well fed or hungry, whether living in plenty or in want. I can do all this through him who gives me strength" (Ephesians 4:12-13).

Discussion Questions:
1. What are some age-appropriate ways you can teach good financial planning to your child(ren)?

2. What are some ways in which you can set a good example in your home in the area of finances (budgeting, adjusting priorities, modeling good decision-making skills, etc.)?

"For God is the one who provides seed for the farmer and then bread to eat. In the same way, he will provide and increase your resources and then produce a great harvest of generosity in you."
2 Corinthians 9:10

Dear God,
Give me wisdom in the area of finances. Help me to make sound financial decisions that will impact my family in positive and long-lasting ways. Let the inheritance that I leave for my child(ren) not be in monetary form only, but also in a rich and healthy knowledge of finances anchored in your Word.
Amen.

Chapter 5: Food

There were two words that we were, under no circumstances, allowed to say when I was growing up: "yuck" and "ewe." My mom taught us that every person has his or her own preferences; but that when we sat down to eat at our family's table, or someone else's table, we needed to eat what was in front of us. If we did not like a certain food, we were allowed to say we "did not care for it," but we were still obligated to eat at least some of it.

My mom always loaded our meals full of fruits and vegetables, as well as healthy proteins and whole grains. We ate our peanut butter and jelly sandwiches on whole wheat bread, and we were expected to eat the crust, too. Our drink choices were mostly water, iced herbal tea, milk, and 100 percent juice. We did not have fruit punch or sodas in the house. We had vegetables on our pizza and dark greens in our salads.

My mom's kitchen was not a restaurant; she was not a short order cook and never would be. She was our mom, and because she was our mom, she took on the responsibility of making sure we ate nutritious food that would help us grow healthy and strong. There was no choice between dark green lettuce and iceberg. We were never asked if we wanted tomatoes on our sandwich; it was assumed that we did. We ate what was served, and if we did not, we were not given an alternative meal. Choosing not to eat meant waiting until the next meal. We ate what my parents ate. There was no kids' food and adults' food in our house. There was only people food.

I am so glad that my mom took such a clear stand when it came to food. Fortunately for us, my mom was and is a very good cook. Still, as a child, I disliked peas, was often not a fan of scrambled eggs, and I most definitely "did not care for" liver. Even so, when my mom served these foods, I ate them, and despite how horrible it was for me in the moment, I guarantee you that I was in no way scarred for life because my parents made me eat my peas. On the contrary, over the years, my preferences have changed, and now I like peas and love scrambled eggs (liver, on the other hand, is a different story). I am so glad that my parents were willing to be unpopular at dinner time in order to teach me good manners and healthy eating habits, both of which have followed me into adulthood.

Discussion Questions:

1. Do you believe your child(ren) eat(s) a healthy, balanced diet?
2. Do your child(ren)'s eating habits fit well within your family norms?
3. Are your child(ren)'s eating habits sustainable?
4. What is working well at mealtimes?

"A person who is full refuses honey,

But even bitter food tastes sweet to the hungry."

-   Proverbs 27:7

Dear God,

Help me to create healthy habits at mealtimes that will nourish and fuel my growing child(ren) and create opportunities for beautiful moments around our family's table. Give me wisdom to create peace at the table as I meet my child(ren)'s immediate need for food, and help me create sustainable and healthy habits that will follow them into adulthood. Give me creative ideas and strategies to teach healthy eating, and give me patience when expectations or attitudes fail. Show me what battles are worth fighting, and show me when I should give grace. Help me to have age-appropriate expectations for my child(ren). Let my attitudes and actions at the table, as well as in life, be motivated by love.

Amen.

Chapter 6: Dating

Turning ten years old in my home was a very special time. Starting at that age, my dad would take us out, individually, for a special birthday dinner date. For my tenth birthday, my dad took me to a fancy Italian restaurant. He told me how beautiful I looked, he opened up the car door for me, and he even ordered me a Shirley Temple to drink. My tenth birthday was very special to me, and so were all of the birthday dinner dates in the years that followed. With each dinner date, my dad instilled value, self-worth and good, old-fashioned chivalry. During these special dinner dates, my dad was not only creating very special memories between the two of us, but he was also acknowledging and honoring the fact that I was growing up. For us girls, our birthday dinner dates were an honored rite of passage, similar to a Quinceañera for Hispanic families.

Another rite of passage that we girls experienced was on the weekend prior to each of us girls starting high school. My parents would sit us down in the living room and talk to us about the importance of our virginity. I remember that on my night, they told me not only about God's desire for me to save myself for my husband, but also for their desire for me to do so. They told me of all the hardship that I could avoid by following God's plan, and they also told me that choices regarding my virginity were not to be made lightly. They told me that society would push me to conform to the world's standards, but that if I made a choice to abstain early on in life, I would see the blessing from that decision for the rest of my life. Having been an audience to the same conversation for my sisters, I already knew what I wanted. I knew that I wanted to save my virginity for my future husband. After I told them my decision, my parents presented me with a beautiful Black Hills gold ring as a sign of the covenant that I had made with God and my parents to remain sexually pure until my wedding night. I wore that ring, which symbolized my covenant, night and day from that point on until my wedding night. Anyone who knew me knew what the ring represented.

My parents taught me that I was valuable. They taught me that who I was as a person, the decisions I made, the values I had, and everything about me, was priceless. When it came to dating, my parents taught me that my company alone was of great value, and that I did not owe any guy anything. My allegiance was to God, my parents and my future husband.

What My Parents Did Right

As we transitioned from girls to young women, my parents set the bar high on how we were to interact with young men. If a young man was interested in dating one of us, he was required to come to the house to ask my parents' permission to do so. My parents told us that any guy not willing to honor us and them in this way was not worth our time. My sisters both dated much earlier than I did, and most of their dates involved inviting the boyfriend to join us for a family dinner that one or both of my sisters had cooked. We were allowed some alone time with our respective boyfriends, but it was in the form of taking a hike together, sitting on the back deck, or working on a project together. Our alone time was always in a communal part of the house or within the community. Boys were never allowed in our rooms, for any reason. When we did go on traditional dates, my parents expected us to say where we were going, what we would be doing, who we would be with and when we would be home. We never saw this as an infringement on our privacy, because my parents modeled this behavior themselves as a sign of respect and honor to each other and us girls. When they went somewhere, they also told us where they were going, what time we should expect them home, and how we could reach them if we needed anything. In our family, considerations like these were a function of honor and respect; it was never about control.

In our home, my parents taught us that it was the young man's role to pursue the girl, not the other way around. For this reason, they did not allow us to call a boy unless it was for a specific reason, such as asking for clarification on a homework assignment or confirming the time or place of an upcoming event. They never allowed us to call a boy "just to talk." My parents taught us that if a boy wanted to talk to us, he would call, and if he did not, then we had better things to do with our time. This phone rule stayed in effect until around the time that we were engaged. Speaking of engagement, that was also something that involved my parents' blessing first.

My parents did not establish these "old fashion" rules for dating to control us, limit our fun, or dictate our lives. They did so to honor, protect, and promote healthy relationships. These rules placed my parents in a position to speak into our lives and provide input based on their observations, wisdom, and life experiences. I am so thankful that my parents created boundaries within our dating relationships, and I am so thankful that I did not fight against them. It is likely that I did not fight against our families' norms for dating because my parents established and taught them long before we technically "needed" them. Because of my parents' forethought and boldness to go against the cultural norms, and because I did not rebel against my parents' rules, I am now reaping the benefits in the form of a very healthy and happy marriage, free from the baggage of multiple broken hearts and soul ties.

Discussion Questions:

1. What were the dating norms in your home growing up? Were they healthy or unhealthy?
2. What expectations do you have for your child(ren) in the realm of dating and relationships? Are they aware of these expectations?
3. How can you partner with your child(ren)/teen(s)/young adult(s) in their future or current dating relationships?

"I pray that your love will overflow more and more, and that you will keep on growing in knowledge and understanding.

For I want you to understand what really matters, so that you may live pure and blameless lives until the day of Christ's return.

May you always be filled with the fruit of your salvation produced in your life by Jesus Christ – for this will bring much glory and praise to God."

-   Philippians 1:9-11

Dear God,

Help me to raise my child(ren) to value integrity and purity. Show me how I can prepare them for healthy relationships, and help me to guide them with love. Let me raise them in such a way that they know their priceless worth and that they will know that they themselves are whole and complete. Help me to teach them that they do not need someone to complete them, because they are already complete in You. Help them to wait for partners who will complement them and the gifts and calling that you have for them.

Amen.

Chapter 7: Manners &
Social Skills

Since I was homeschooled, my mom was our teacher across the board for most of our grammar school years. I personally was homeschooled from my second-grade year up until the end of my freshman year of high school. During this time, my mom taught us all the basics: math, history, science, and language arts. My mom was a great teacher, and she always went above and beyond the basic curriculum. In addition to teaching us the basics, my mom also taught us how to cook, do household chores, and even how to do some basic sewing.

Obviously, all of these things are important, but there is another subject that she taught us that I think is just as important, and that is manners. As a young girl, I remember my mom sitting us three girls down at the dining room table and teaching us how to eat with proper etiquette. She taught us to put our napkins in our laps, she taught us which forks to use and when, and she even taught us how to spit a piece of gristle or bone into our napkins (making it look as though we were just wiping our mouths, so that we would not offend anyone at the table). When our family had guests over for dinner, my mom would always prepare us on how to be good hostesses. She taught us to offer to take our guests' coats and offer them something to drink. She taught us how to give directions to the bathroom. (In fact, she taught us how to give driving directions, too, by using the appropriate words, such as "left" and "right," instead of just pointing and assuming that the driver could read our minds.) My mom also taught us to watch our guests toward the end of dinner, and to look for signs that they were done eating. If a guest was done, she taught us that we should then get up and politely ask if we could clear his or her plate. We would do this until all the plates were cleared, and then we would serve the dessert. My mom taught us to go beyond the basic etiquette of "please" and "thank you." She taught us to serve our guests and one another out of love, honor and respect.

I also remember my mom sitting us down on several different occasions and teaching us girls how to treat each other. While we were still young girls, my mom told us that someday, boys would start to call us, and that when this began happening, we would be tempted to tease each other. My mom taught us that jokes were only funny if everyone was laughing, and that it was not right to say or do things to embarrass each other. She taught us to be more than just sisters, but also to be friends, and to lift each other up, not tear one another down. If we could not get along with our own family members, she said, we would have little hope of getting along with people outside of the home.

My mom not only taught us how to be a good hostess and family member, but my parents also taught us how to be a good guest. When we got to the age that we were being invited to go out to eat with friends and their family, we were taught to ask our host what they suggested on the menu or ask them what they were going to order. That way we would have an idea of what the appropriate price range would be, so we were sure to not wear out our welcome by ordering something too expensive, nor were we offending our host by ordering too little.

When it came to situations in which we would be interacting with new people--whether it was selling Girl Scout cookies, calling a new friend to invite her over, or asking for the manager when one of us was looking for her first job--my mom would always have us practice conversations with her. She would role play the person with whom we would be talking, and she would have us practice what we would say. While at times it felt weird to role play telephone calls or job interviews, the reality is that it was a great tool that helped us to practice being confident and respectful so that we were presenting ourselves as mature, well-mannered young women. My mom would even have us practice leaving a message on an answering machine. She taught us to speak up, to speak slowly, and to repeat our names and phone number twice during the message so that listeners would not become frustrated having to replay the message to get the entire number down.

The life skills that my parents taught my sisters and I when it came to treating people with honor and respect are priceless to me. I am blessed to have many wonderful, lifelong relationships with family members and non-family members--both personal and professional--that have matured and grown over the years into such beautiful friendships. I believe that these wonderful friendships have developed the way that they have because of the foundation my parents laid in teaching us how to treat other people.

Discussion Questions:

1. How are good manners used in your home to promote healthy relationships in and out of the home?
2. Have you ever used role playing to help your child(ren) practice a new life skill? If not, what is stopping you?
3. How does teaching manners through hospitality expand your child(ren)'s social skills?

"Love each other with genuine affection, and take delight in honoring each other. Never be lazy, but work hard and serve the Lord enthusiastically.

Rejoice in our confident hope. Be patient in trouble, and keep on praying.

When God's people are in need, be ready to help them.

Always be eager to practice hospitality."

-    Romans 12:10-13

Dear God,

Help me to raise my child(ren) to honor others with thoughtful kindness. Help me to lead by my own actions and attitudes. Let our family be known for being people of honor and hospitality. Let our behavior reflect our mindfulness of others and our desire to be motivated by love always.

Amen.

Chapter 8: God at Home

I am extremely blessed by the fact that I was raised in a Christian home. Throughout my entire life, my parents have shown by example what it truly means to be a Christian. Growing up, it was normal to read the Bible as a family; it was normal to pray together, and not just at meal times; and it was normal to include God in every part of life, not just at church on Sundays. It was also normal to hear my dad pray for a friend over the phone, to hear the answer to prayer soon afterward, and to hear my dad give the glory to God. It was normal to see my mom's eyes tear up as she worshiped God in church or at Christian gatherings. It was normal when we had guests over to join hands together before they departed, to thank God for the time of fellowship, and to pray a blessing over them. It was normal to fall asleep to the sound of my parents saying their own prayers in bed together, which included hearing each one of our names being lifted up to God in love. It was normal to see and feel God moving in our lives.

Many people have amazing stories of how they came to be a Christian. I love hearing my dad's testimony, and especially how he tells it with passion and excitement. Even after more than 45 years, each time he tells it, it is obvious that it truly was a moment that totally changed the course of his life. From this foundational moment, my dad and mom built their relationship and our family culture around the understanding that God is real, tangible and active in our lives.

My parents' example of faith in our home affected my salvation. My story is not like the typical "come-to-Jesus" story. I cannot tell you what I was wearing, or where I was, or even how old I was when I prayed "the prayer." What I can tell you is that I cannot remember a time in which I did not know Jesus. Because of my parents' example in our home, God has always been real to me, and I have never doubted His love, His power, and His divinity. While I realize that every person must make a decision to follow Christ on his or her own, I believe my faith was birthed out of the culture that my parents established in our home. They seemed to have the revelation of God's truth that few seem to have, and because I witnessed this, even at a very young age, I was able to understand that God is both tangible and personal.

Knowing God and knowing that Jesus died on the cross is not something I needed to rationalize. The reality of God's existence was simple and normal for me, and it still is. In our home, there was no kid-sized God and adult-sized God, and Christianity certainly wasn't something to practice when I got older. Faith in God was a part of my life from the beginning.

I am so glad that my parents included God in our daily lives, that they introduced my sisters and me to Jesus at a young age, and that they encouraged us to pursue the gifts of the Holy Spirit as children. In the same way that a young child does not doubt when her parents tell her that the sky is blue, I never had any reason to doubt the realness of God. Just like the color blue is accepted and learned through consistent examples time after time, so the reality of God was made evident daily in the lives of my parents and in my own heart. Their example of how to follow Christ was and is a constant gift of love to me and an anchor in hard times.

I was probably about six years old when I was baptized in a small creek, along with my sisters and some other adults who had recently become Christians. My dad, although not a pastor, was the one who baptized us. I am so thankful that my dad recognized his role as the priest of our family and took the initiative to baptize us. I must admit that at the time of my baptism, I did not really understand all the symbolism of baptism: dying with Christ, being resurrected with Christ, sins being washed away, etc.

What I did understand is that baptism was a way that you show God and others that you have accepted Jesus in your heart and that you want to grow and live in Him. For me, that was enough. I am so glad that my parents recognized my desire to grow in my walk with Jesus from a young age, and that they did not hinder me from doing so based on my age.

Discussion Questions:

1. Where (church, school, home) are Christian influences found in your child(ren)'s life?
2. Do you feel comfortable bringing God's perspective into everyday conversations?
3. In what ways can God's presence be seen in your home and in your child(ren)'s world?
4. What do you do when your child(ren) asks questions about God or life and you don't know the answer?

"Train up a child in the way he should go,

And when he is old he will not depart from it."

- Proverbs 22:6 (NKJV)

Dear God,

Help me to live my faith every day. Let my child(ren) not only be an audience to my faith, but also active in their own. Let your love and presence be tangible in our home in an undeniable way. Help me to make our home a temple for your presence and a place where righteousness, peace and love abound. Let our home be a place of miracles and a place where your Word is active and living. Let my love for You be contagious. Be the Lord of my life, my family and my world.

Amen.

My sisters and I were all homeschooled for the majority of our grammar school years, and I personally was homeschooled from second grade through ninth grade. Being homeschooled allowed us girls the opportunity not only to learn the normal reading, writing and arithmetic, but it also gave us the freedom to dive into other subjects and projects, such as music lessons, dance, sports, cooking, basic sewing, raising animals, woodworking, and art.

I am so thankful to my parents for all that they sacrificed so that we could be homeschooled. My parents chose to homeschool us prior to the creation of charter schools and homeschool vouchers, and they purchased all of our textbooks with their own money. My mom taught us all the subjects, and at times even hired tutors to ensure that we were getting the best education possible. Our school day started around 8:00 a.m. sitting at the kitchen counter for Bible reading and then prayer. From there, we jumped into our studies. Our days had structure. However, we were also given the flexibility to work at our own pace. In general, we were able to get through lessons much more quickly than we would have been able to in a traditional school, and often, we were done with the academic work by around twelve or one o'clock. This gave us the rest of the afternoon for practicing the piano, cooking, or working on other projects. By the time our friends were getting out of school, we had accomplished everything they had, plus more.

While in many ways we may have seemed like the stereotypical homeschool family, my parents did several things that went above and beyond typical. My mom made sure that even though we were homeschooled, we had plenty of opportunities for making friends and socializing. As kids, we were involved in AWANAs, 4-H, dance classes, various church activities, and basketball camps. In fact, you name it, and we were probably doing it. My parents were not homeschooling us so that we could be our own little secret Christian society, hidden from the world, which seems to be the perception many people have of homeschooling. Instead, they homeschooled us so that we could both have the best education possible and so that we could be brought up firmly in our Christian faith. They also did not homeschool us as a way to hide us from the world. They homeschooled us because, at the time, it was the best education option available to us. Homeschooling was the environment in which we were all provided an opportunity to excel, and that made it the best choice for us.

While my parents are obviously firm believers in homeschooling, they never acted as though it was the "only option". From year to year, my parents looked at all the education options available to them, and then chose the best one for each of us girls.

When my sisters and I started high school, there were only two options: homeschooling and public school. This was due to the fact that the nearest private school was about one-and-a-half hours away from where we lived. At this time, my sisters were both at an age when they wanted more independence, and like a lot of teenagers, they just needed some space. As a result, public school was their best option, and they both did very well. For me, though, I just was not ready for a traditional school in ninth grade, so homeschooling one more year proved to be beneficial to me. However, during the summer between my ninth-grade year and tenth-grade year, we moved to a larger city where there were more options. Again, my parents looked into all the options available and chose a private Christian high school, where I excelled, earning Principal's Honor Roll, and where I participated in multiple clubs and served in student council.

I am so glad that my parents took the road less traveled and were willing and able to homeschool us girls for most of our elementary and junior high years. The things that we learned while being homeschooled, and the experiences we were able to have, are priceless to me, and I know they are very valuable to my sisters, as well.

Discussion Questions:

1. What options do you feel you have when it comes to your child(ren)'s education (public, private, charter, magnet, homeschool, online)?
2. What are the most important factors for you when choosing a school (academics, extracurricular activities, Christian vs. secular, class size, etc.)?
3. How has God given you peace in your educational choices for your child(ren)?

"Do you see a man who excels in his work?

He will stand before kings;

He will not stand before unknown men."

- Proverbs 22:29

Dear God,

Give me wisdom and knowledge when it comes to my child(ren)'s education. Help me to know how best to meet their needs. Help me to instill in my child(ren) a love for learning and a thirst for knowledge. Help me to choose the best educational setting for my child(ren) and to have your peace about my decision. I entrust my child(ren) to you, and I ask that you protect them and keep them from harm. Place them with teachers who will see the worth that you have instilled in them. Surround them with friends who will raise them up, not pull them down. Help them to learn the value of hard work and not to give up when things get hard.

Amen.

*O*ne thing that I have always been thankful for, even as a kid, is that my parents disciplined me. This is not to say that I enjoyed being disciplined. Obviously, no one does. I was, however, always glad that my parents not only taught me right from wrong, but also taught and modeled appropriate behavior. My parents laid down a firm line for what was acceptable for us to do and what would happen if we were to cross that line. Within our family, discipline was not simply the act of being punished for misbehavior. Instead, discipline was a set of clear expectations, followed by clear outcomes. In the novel *Love Finds a Home*, by Janett Oake, one of the characters states, "Discipline needs to be consistent...or it is not discipline – only punishment." This quote is a perfect example of discipline in our home. Discipline was the enforcement of clear and consistent boundaries with predictable outcomes if we crossed them.

One area in which my parents always expected us to behave appropriately was while going into public places. If we were going into a store that might have breakable things, my mom or dad would always tell us that this was a store where we needed to keep our hands in our pockets and look only with our eyes. When going into a grocery store, my mom would tell us what things she was going to get and how she expected us to participate. She might say something like this:

> "We are going into the grocery store to get some food. We are in a hurry today, so I need to stick to my list and get in and out as quickly as possible. I need all of you to stay right with me the entire time. When we get to the register, I will need your help putting the groceries up on the counter for the clerk."

or

> "We need to get some things for the barbecue this weekend. Once we get done with what is on my list, you girls can help me pick out what we will have for dessert."

My mom and dad set clear expectations for what would be happening and how we would be participating. When it came to teaching us how to act, my parents also used every teachable moment that they could find. If we were at a store and another child near us was throwing a fit, my mom or dad would quietly say something like this:

"How is that child acting right now?
Is his behavior appropriate?"

"Wow. That child is being very rude
and disrespectful to her mom. What do
you think her mom should do?"

"I am so glad that I have young ladies
who know it's not okay to run through the
store."

All of these questions and statements led us girls to the only logical explanation: the child needed discipline. In our home, discipline was not an expression of anger and helplessness, but was a part of a logical chain of events. If we did something wrong, we would be corrected. Whether it was a spanking, an early bedtime, extra chores, or often in my case, an unwanted nap, the discipline was just part of a chain of events that occurred when we chose to disobey.

My most memorable time of being disciplined was when I was around five years old. I was at the age when I was no longer supposed to be sucking my thumb, but occasionally, I would still do it. I remember being in my sister's bedroom, sucking my thumb while playing. I heard my mom call out to me, asking if I was sucking my thumb. Thinking that my mom was in the kitchen, and could not see me, I yelled back an answer of "no." I don't think I even bothered to take my thumb out of my mouth as I answered. The reality was that my mom was not in the kitchen at all, but had been watching me from around the corner the entire time. I was caught red handed. My mom immediately called me out on my lie and told me that there was only one thing that could be done with a tongue that told lies. I was ushered to the bathroom, where my tongue got a good taste of some Irish Spring® soap. To this day, I can remember the taste and the smell of Irish Spring® soap. That was my first and only time of ever having my mouth washed out with soap, but it most definitely left an impression. While, at times, I have thought that sucking my thumb was a pretty dumb thing to get caught lying about, the truth was that I had, in fact, lied. In our home, discipline was not reserved only for the really big stuff. Disobedience and dishonesty were wrong no matter what the context was, and we knew that if we got caught--which we always did--there would be discipline to follow.

Even though I never enjoyed being sent to my room, sent to bed, or spanked, one thing that I did look forward to was the first few minutes after the correction had been delivered. My mom or dad would often pick me up and set me on their knee while they told me how much they loved me and how it pained them to have to discipline me. It was a time of putting things back to how they belonged. Truth be told, oftentimes, what I had done I could not undo, but together, we would work out a plan of what I could do differently the next time. Once the correction had been given, this post-conversation would ensure a restored relationship, and life would go back to normal.

I was always glad that my parents did not drag out punishments, or again and again bring up the things that we had done wrong. Sometimes, I would hear my friends' parents openly sharing about all the things that their kids had done wrong that day or that week. I always felt bad for them, because to me, the embarrassment of being repeatedly reminded of the incident would have been far worse than the timeout or other form of correction that had been given. I remember my sisters and I once saying that if we were going to do something bad, we should do it early in the day. This way, the crime and the punishment would be long forgotten by the time dad got home from work. Of course, we were joking, but there was a truth to our kidding. Even though we knew that my parents did not keep secrets from each other, we always hoped that our mess-ups would somehow be forgotten during the course of the day. It was embarrassing for us to have our dad hear about something we had done while he was at work, but it would have been far worse to have had our "incident" advertised to everyone who called or came over. My parents respected our privacy and advertised only our strengths, not our shortcomings.

** I want to be clear that my parents never beat me or abused me in any way. They may have spanked me a few times, but these were isolated and limited events and were not my parents' go-to form of correction. In most cases, they gave me a "time-out" by telling me I needed to stand in the corner and "think about what I had done."

Discussion Questions:

1. Is discipline consistent in your home?
2. Are you and your spouse in agreement on how to discipline?

3. After you correct your child(ren),, how do you mend the relationship again?

"Children, obey your parents in the Lord, for this is right.

'Honor your father and mother' – which is the first commandment with a promise – 'so that it may go well with you and that you may enjoy long life on the earth.'

Fathers, do not exasperate your children; instead, bring them up in the training and instruction of the Lord."

-   Ephesians 6:1-4

Dear God,

Help me to discipline my child(ren) in love. Give me patience and grace as I raise them to be kind and to honor others. Give me wisdom to know how best to correct my child(ren) in a way that molds their character, without crushing their spirit. Keep my anger in check, and help me to correct from a place of love, not wrath. Give my child(ren) a heart that is sensitive to knowing right from wrong, and give them a desire to choose the paths of righteousness, peace and joy.

Amen.

My parents were always very involved in our lives. While we all had our individual interests, we did things as a family. We all listened to the same songs in the car, most often the local Christian radio station. We had one TV, and when we watched it, we watched it as a family in the living room. My parents were always very conscientious about what we were listening to and watching. When watching movies that we had rented, it was common to fast-forward if there was an intimate bedroom scene, or a particularly violent scene. My parents used these fast-forward moments again and again to instill our family's values. Growing up, my parents established early on that a man and woman should never "sleep" with each other unless they were married. While this was a standard of our Christian faith, it was also a matter of good choices and using wisdom. In the movies that we watched, and the stories that we heard, there was almost always heartache and pain caused by doing things "in the wrong order."

My parents shielded us from scary movies and TV shows. If our favorite family sitcom or drama was having a spooky Halloween episode, we would shut off the TV and find another activity to enjoy. My parents taught us to guard our hearts, minds and eyes from unnecessary violence, and taught that fear was not entertaining.

I remember the first and only time I watched a scary movie. I was at a sleepover, and it was a movie that I had heard about over and over again at my Christian high school. I figured that it was okay to watch because I was with other Christians. To this day, when I think of this night, I still want to wash my eyes out with soap. I had never seen anything so gruesome or horrifying. I realized that night that I was different from my friends, and I also realized that I did not mind being different. I understood that over time, people become desensitized to violence and destruction, and I also realized that I did not want to be one of those people. From that day forward, I no longer needed my parents to monitor my movies, because I was glad to do it myself. I was glad--and I still am--that my parents sheltered me from violent and scary images, and I know that I never wanted to call such a thing "entertainment."

As we girls grew older and started to have our own preferences in music, my parents were careful to listen to and/or have us tell them what the lyrics were to the songs. They told us that it was not enough just to enjoy the beat and musicality of a song, but that we also needed to protect our ears by choosing only songs with lyrics that had uplifting and life-giving messages.

Even though my parents did not share our love of Christian alternative rock music and Christian hip hop, they went to great inconveniences to drive us and our friends to concerts, supporting our choice in Christian music. They provided ample opportunity for us to have fun throughout our teen years, allowing us to jump around in the mosh pits while they themselves stayed in the back with their ear plugs securely in place.

Discussion Questions:

1. How do you monitor your child(ren)'s screen/media time?
2. What standards has your family established when it comes to what you watch/listen to?
3. Do you yourself follow your family's standards?

"Above all else, guard your heart, for everything you do flows from it."

- Proverbs 4:23

"Finally, brothers and sisters, whatever is true, whatever is noble, whatever is right, whatever is pure, whatever is lovely, whatever is admirable – if anything is excellent or praiseworthy – think about such things."

- Philippians 4:8

Dear God,

Give me wisdom to guard my child(ren)'s heart(s). Help me to be their gatekeeper in such a way that they both embrace my protection and learn to self-govern to protect their own heart(s). Help me to set the example with my own life by protecting my own heart, too. Help me to seek out entertainment that is life-giving and life-building for myself and my family.

Amen.

Chapter 12: Secrets

There were things that, as a child, I never knew about my parents: hurts that they faced as children and young adults, and mistakes that they made. Some aspects of my parents' lives were purposely kept in the past.

While we were growing up, my parents often told us that they always wanted to be honest with us. This was actually the reason that they chose not to introduce the traditions of Santa Claus and the Easter Bunny. They never wanted my sisters and me to doubt what they told us to be true.

Honesty is such a crucial component of healthy parent-child relationships. If a child cannot trust what his or her parents have told that child to be true, there is no foundation. How can a relationship grow without a foundation?

Telling the truth in any relationship is paramount. In my life, however, I have learned that being honest and being transparent are not always the same thing. I have seen other parents' dedication to an open and honest relationship come at the cost of wisdom and their children's best interest. Parents who desire a best-friend relationship with their children often rob those children of their innocence and childhood. I remember a friend coming to me in tears, telling me that her mother had just told her that she was thinking of getting a divorce. The mother had not even told her own husband yet. Another friend I grew up with heard his mother openly talk about getting abortions: "I'll be late picking you up from school on Friday because I have an appointment to get an abortion," his mom said. I heard other parents openly joke that their child was an accident, saying, "We didn't want to have any more kids, but you came along anyway."

Just because something is true does not make it edifying; and just because your child is mature compared to his or her peers does not make that child an adult. My parents set a high standard within our family for truth, but this did not equate to full transparency.

While we were growing up, my parents told us stories about their lives prior to them having children, and also prior to them meeting each other. My mom, who was a Christian from a young age, told us about different Sunday school teachers and neighbors who positively impacted her life. She told us about fun times she had at church camp and stories about going swimming in the summer. She told us about her first few jobs and about how she put herself through college. She also told us about how difficult it was for her as a single, young woman in the 1970s to be taken seriously by banks, real estate agents, and businessmen when she was preparing to open her own successful preschool business. My mom told us about first meeting my dad, and how she initially turned down his requests to take her out on a date (he smoked, she said, and he dated a lot of different girls). Still, while my mom told us a lot about her childhood and young adult years, she did not tell us everything.

Even my dad, whom we knew grew up in a non-Christian home, purposely told us only the 'G'-rated stories of his childhood. We always knew that my mom had practically threatened his life if he ever told us about some of the pranks he pulled as a kid and adolescent. We knew that my dad had a past. We knew that he was not a Christian when he grew up, and as a result, we knew that he had not been taught the Biblical values of saving one's sexual purity for one's spouse. My dad told us time and time again about how he wished someone would have told him to save himself for his future wife. Yes, my dad did tell us some of his secrets, but he limited what he told us to those things that would help us avoid the mistakes he had made. In other words, he used his past for our good.

My sisters and I used to love to look through my parents' wedding album and ask them questions about their wedding, about how they met, and about all the other details that girls love to know. My mom had made her dress, and it was beautiful. It was a pink dress with pastel flowers, and in my mind, this was the most beautiful and stylish 1970s wedding dress ever. My dad wore a white tuxedo with a pink carnation (my mom's favorite flower); and my dad also had just a hint of a mustache, something that, based on the stories, he worked long and hard on. Everything about my parents' story was perfect, from their first date--which also ended up being the day my dad got saved--to their wedding day and beyond.

Fast-forward to adulthood.

About six months after my husband Bruce and I were married, my parents invited my sisters and their husbands, as well as Bruce and me, to their house for the weekend. Saturday morning, while I was helping my mom with breakfast, my dad came and gave me a hug and said, "How did we get so blessed to have such wonderful girls?" My reply was that we girls were equally blessed to have such wonderful parents. To my surprise, my dad became very somber and said, "Well, we're not perfect. We have made our mistakes." It was very unusual for my dad to say something like this, and I assured him that, in my mind, they were great parents.

After breakfast, my parents asked us to gather in the living room, and they both got very serious. My sisters and I all got scared, because we had never seen them like this. We weren't sure if one of them was dying, if they were having marital problems, or what. My parents then began to tell us about their past.

My dad was in the Coast Guard during Vietnam, and during one of his leaves back home, he met and married a girl in a whirlwind romance. He returned to his duties thinking that he had it all, including a tattoo--which, of course, all sailors had to have-- and a wife waiting for him at home. He now had someone to return home to, but was devastated when his next leave came. It was then that he found that his "wife" had only married him to make her ex-boyfriend jealous, that they were now back together, and that she was living with her boyfriend. As a result, my dad's marriage was annulled by a judge.

During this same time period, my mom-- most likely in desperation to get out of her parents' house-- met and quickly married a man. According to my mom, immediately after they married, this man became very cruel and abusive. Unsure of what to do, she also went before a judge to find out what her options were, and the judge quickly annulled the marriage.

Never once did my parents lie to us about their past; they just chose instead to protect us from it by not volunteering all the information. When my parents told us about their pasts, and the fact that they had both been married prior to finding each other, we were all just so relieved that no one was dying that I really don't think any of us really cared.

I believe that my parents used great wisdom in keeping their pasts hidden from us until an appropriate time. My parents were always very protective of us girls when it came to boys, and if we had known about their pasts, we probably would have used their pasts as leverage every time we thought they were being too strict or overprotective. We probably would have foolishly told them that they were "just being overprotective" because they did not want us to repeat their mistakes. My parents wanted us to be raised in an environment where marriage was seen as a lifetime commitment. It was for this reason that they waited until we were all grown and happily married before they told of their pasts.

How my parents were able to get their entire families not to mention their pasts is nothing short of a miracle. My mom said that she was always afraid that one of us girls would ask her why she did not have a white wedding dress; but thanks to our understanding of the 1970s, we just all assumed a pink pastel dress was the norm.

I am glad that my parents purposely omitted the fact that they had both previously been married. I truly believe that they did this for our benefit. My heart breaks to know that they both went through such pain while they were in their early 20s, but I am thankful that they did not pass their pain onto us girls.

I know that many of you parents who may be reading this may have your own regrets, and in some cases, there is no escaping the reality of your past. Unfortunately, we do live in a fallen world full of broken relationships, abuse and crimes of many kinds. The purpose of this chapter is not to encourage you to bury your troubles in the sand like an ostrich buries his head. Instead, it is to encourage you to pray and ask God how you can spare your children from the weight of burdens that they were never meant to bear. Always be honest and use wisdom when revealing hard truths.

Discussion Questions:

1. Are there things from your past that should stay in your past?
2. How do you navigate tough topics with your child(ren)?

3. Can your child(ren) count on you for an honest answer?
4. Are the boundaries you have in your life built for your protection or for your child(ren)'s sake?

"Discretion will protect you, and understanding will guard you."

- Proverbs 2:11

"Set a guard over my mouth, Lord; keep watch over the door of my lips."

- Psalms 141:3

Dear God,

Give me wisdom to know what to share and when to share with my child(ren) the hard truths from my life. Help my sharing of hard truths be for their edification and benefit, and not accidental slips of the tongue. Help me to have purpose and love when I reveal to my child(ren) some of life's many imperfections. Help my words shape their life/lives in positive ways so that they may be able to avoid my most regrettable moments.

Amen.

Chapter 13: Sisters

Being the youngest in my family, I not only had two amazing parents who cared for me, but I also was fortunate enough to have two older sisters who have always truly loved me. To be honest, I really don't know how much of my relationship with my sisters is the result of us all sharing the same great parents and how much is just a result of me being extra blessed. I am almost five years younger than my oldest sister Lacie, and two years younger than my sister Glory, but for the majority of my years growing up, age never seemed to matter.

I have a picture of myself as a baby, sitting in a doll high chair, being "fed" imaginary food by my oldest sister Lacie, who was apparently "playing house." This picture truly captures the love and tenderness that both my sisters showered on me as a child, and still shower on me to this day. My sisters were always looking out for me – even to the point that, at times, it felt like I had three moms. The many memories that I have with both of my sisters are too numerous to count and too wonderful for mere words to do them justice. I remember that, as a little kid, my sisters would invite me to join them in the things that they were doing. As a kid, this was just normal; but now that I am grown, I realize that it is not always the norm to have older siblings wanting their younger sibling hanging around.

While my two sisters are both amazing women, they are almost polar opposites in their talents, interests, and personalities. I always seemed just to fit right in the middle. In fact, I had the best of both worlds. I remember going on countless horseback rides with my sister Lacie and being her sidekick when she was training animals. I also remember the countless makeovers that my sister Glory gave me and the care that she took in looking out for me. Both of my sisters taught me life lessons through their love for me and their willingness to allow me to be truly a part of their lives.

To my sister Lacie, thank you for teaching me how to ride a horse, for taking me on buggy rides, inviting me to hang out with you and your friends, and for letting me be a part of your everyday life. You were always there to hang out with me and you never made me feel like a baby or a tag-a-long. Thank you for all the stories that you read to me and the stories that you made up for me while I would lay on your bed and just listen. To this day, I still love to listen to stories. My love for stories is most likely the reason that I became a history teacher. Even though you left for college while I was only 12 years old, you didn't forget about me. I fondly remember the letters you would write to me and the many times that you would call me just to talk. Even though we are both adults and you are busy with a husband, five kids, and a farm, you still make time to call me just to talk. Thank you.

To my sister Glory, thank you for being such a big part of my life. I remember once mom had given me the chore of sweeping all the pine needles off the deck (I was probably about eight years old and you were probably about ten). I thought that I was being very clever by sweeping most of the pine needles under the table instead of off the deck, but you came out and told me that I needed to do the job right. I remember asking you why, thinking that no one would know the difference; but you told me, "*I would know the difference.*" That day, you taught me a lesson that has stuck with me ever since. You taught me to take pride in my own work and to do a good job even when no one is looking. After telling me all of this, you went a step further and helped me to pull out the bench from the picnic table so that I could get the pine needles back out and do the job right. Another memory that I have with you brings tears to my eyes every time I think of it (even as I write this now, my eyes are watering). This memory is of when you and I both were in high school. I was an underclassman who was most definitely out of place in every way, and you were my cool upperclassman sister. I'd had a bad day, week, month - and was really at a rough transition in life. It was after school, and we had just met up to go meet mom out at the car. While we were walking through the locker corridor, you stopped me and said, "Hey, look, a penny." I looked down, and to my dismay, I saw that the penny was tails up. I said something sarcastic, like, "Oh, great. It's tails." It's not that I had ever believed in luck or superstition, but it just seemed to me like more proof that I was having a bad day. As you scooped up the penny and put it into your hand, you said, "No, when it is tails, it is a good thing, too. When it is tails, you are supposed to give it to a friend." I immediately began to think of all of your friends and started to wonder which one of them would get the penny. Just then, you handed the penny to me, put your arm around my shoulder, and just kept walking, as though nothing had happened. Ever since that day, every time I see a coin that is tails up, I think of you and how such a simple act has made such a powerful difference in my life. From that day, I was no longer just the sister of one of the coolest and prettiest girls in school, but I also became her valued friend.

I am blessed to have two loving sisters who also are two of my closest friends. My mom and dad always used to tell us that, as sisters, we needed to value each other because we would never have a friend like a sister. To me, there is more truth to their counsel than even they knew. I have truly been blessed beyond measure.

Discussion Questions:

1. What was your experience growing up with siblings? Was it positive or negative?
2. How can you promote healthy relationships within your family unit for your child(ren)?
3. In what ways do you teach your child(ren) to value not only the similarities that they share with others, but their differences, as well?

"A friend loves at all times, and a brother is born for a time of adversity."

- Proverbs 17:17

Dear God,

Help me to raise not only siblings, but friends. Help me to create a culture of honor in our home where we raise each other up instead of tearing each other down. Help me to teach my child(ren) to place value on each person's strengths and to cover each other's weaknesses. Give me wisdom when childhood disputes arise. Help me to mediate in a way that produces honor, grace, and love, and not in a way that produces winners and losers.

May my child(ren) always feel safety and love within our family unit.

Amen.

Chapter 14: Leaving a Legacy

At this point in this book, I think it is very clear that I had a great childhood. My parents created a beautiful, safe, and loving environment for me to grow. They raised me with love, wisdom and lots of prayer. My sisters and I are all grown and married, with kids of our own now. We are all successful within our own individual endeavors, and my parents now have the opportunity to love on twelve grandchildren, ages five to nineteen.

I am no longer a child. I am a parent now. It is a role that my husband and I take very seriously. We are incredibly thankful that God has honored us with the stewardship of five beautiful children. The responsibility of raising up Godly children who are confident in who they are and the giftings God has given them lies upon us. The task of teaching our children to love others like Jesus loves is ours. The responsibility of raising children who will someday be contributing members of society belongs to none other than us. All that said, with our children, some days it seems like our main goals revolve around simpler, more fundamental things. This includes things like keeping them fed and clothed; limiting screen time; and providing opportunities for good, old-fashioned play time (today we made and then flew paper airplanes).

I am blessed. When it comes to being a parent, I feel like my own parents created a really great foundation upon which my husband and I could build. I not only have my childhood memories to build from, but I also have both my parents and my sisters, just a phone call away. Not everyone has these resources within his or her family. My parents did not have these resources.

Whether you find yourself like me, with a wealth of resources at your disposal, or whether you-- like my parents-- have more what-not-to-do's, in your tool box, our obligation and responsibility to our children is the same. With God's help, we *all* can raise awesome kids who, like me, will be able to look back on their childhoods with fond memories.

Because I did have such a great and healthy childhood, my husband and I do feel a responsibility to continue the work that was begun, through building upon the foundations we were given. For us, parenting is about building a multigenerational legacy of health and love. Our prayer is that our children will grow up to have an even greater and healthier spirit, soul, and

body than we do, *and* that *their* children will also
surpass them. We continually pray that our ceiling will
be our children's floor. To us, this means that our
victories will be their starting places.

Spiritually, this means that we do not have to wait
for the kids to be "older" to explain and expose them to
spiritual truths. Based on my own experiences as a
young child, I know that my love for and understanding
of God was genuine at a young age, and so we greatly
encourage our children to pray, talk to God, and expect
God to do the impossible (this includes praying for lost
fidget spinners to be found). When our four year-old
told us that he sees angels, we did not roll our eyes and
assume he had an overactive imagination. We instead
told him to say 'Hi." When our six year-old began
expressing interest in being baptized, we didn't just
dismiss it; we took the time to listen to him and taught
him what the Bible says on the subject. When he
continued to express a desire for baptism, we realized
that this was not just a whim on his part, but a genuine
desire to be baptized. That summer, we organized a
baptism celebration at our home; and we invited our
son's friends, church family, relatives and neighbors to
be witnesses as my husband and our children's pastor
baptized him. It was such a beautiful day and memory
for our entire family.

Not only do we want our children to be equipped in their intellect, but we also want them to have the emotional intelligence to know their identity and to build relationships based on truth and love. To the best of our ability, we want to be motivated by love in everything that we do so that our children can inherit a spirit of love and not a spirit of fear.

One example of my effort to make this true has come on the freeway. Freeway driving, in fact, has never been my favorite activity. On a good traffic day, I can feel my body tense up, and I repeatedly have to encourage my inner mind and body to relax. Prior to having children, I used to tell my husband that I hated driving next to the construction blockades that are built right on the edges of the lanes, because it made me feel unsafe. I also told him that I didn't like driving behind the shiny metallic fuel trucks because I found that seeing my car's reflection in the metal was distracting. One day, prior to having our first child, my husband told me that I needed to stop speaking my fears. At first, I did not understand what he meant, but he went on to explain. The driving lane, he said, was the same size with or without the blockades bordering it, and I was perfectly capable of driving safely whether surrounded by blockade borders or shiny fuel trucks. He said that, soon, we would have children in the car, and he did not want me passing my fears on to our children. To some of you, this might seem extreme, but to me, it really made sense. As a result, I work very hard not to vocalize my fears around my children. Away from the freeway, this has meant suppressing the shrieks and fanfare while catching the lizard that tried to make our pantry its home, even though I was totally freaking out inside.   Having the desire for my ceiling to be my children's floor means that my fears do not need to be their fears.

Growing up, my husband and I were either homeschooled or we attended private Christian schools, and neither of these had school dances.   When we were invited to a few dances in high school and college, we were so limited in our experience that we both held back and became wall flowers, especially for the fast songs. It was not until years after we were married, when we were invited to be bridesmaids and groomsmen in wedding parties, that we realized how much fun we had missed, due to our own insecurities. Now, when we attend weddings or cultural events, we join in the fun, and we bring our children out on the dance floor with us. Neither of us are great dancers, but we are at a place in life where we do not want to let our fears or insecurities dictate what we can and cannot do. We want our children's inheritance to be one of courage and freedom. This is what we want to pass onto them.

Discussion Questions:

1. What are ways in which you want your child(ren) to exceed you?
2. In what ways can you turn your fears into opportunities to speak life?
3. How can you foster growth in your child(ren), especially in areas where you feel weak?

"For physical training is of some value, but godliness has value for all things, holding promise for both the present life and the life to come."

- 1 Timothy 4:8

"For the Spirit God gave us does not make us timid, but gives us power, love and self-discipline."

- 2 Timothy 1:7

Dear God,

Help me to raise my child(ren) to be unlimited by my limitations, and to reach out boldly for everything you created them for. Give me the courage to speak life, even in the face of my fears. Fill me with your love overflowing, and let this be my child(ren)'s inheritance.

Amen.

Chapter 15: Core Values

With multi-generational health and wholeness in mind, my husband and I have three core values that we have borrowed and made our own from people we admire. A core value, similar to a family crest or banner, is like a cinematic theme song that plays again and again. Most people can easily recognize and identify even small clips of the theme songs from movies like *Rocky*, *Jurassic Park*, *Star Wars*, etc. It is our prayer that our core values will be the theme song to our lives and that, like a compass, they will guide us on our journey as we set out to live our best lives, to glorify our loving God and to raise the coming generations to do the same.

I have the desire to share our core values not because I think you need to adopt them for yourselves-- although you are welcome to do so--but, more importantly, because I believe sharing the things that *we* are passionate about will help others to discover the things that *they* are passionate about. In the Bible, in First Corinthians, chapter twelve, the apostle Paul talks about us all being different parts of the same body. The sooner that we can discover and embrace the *part* that we are, the better we are suited for working together in unity, from a healthy place.

These are our core values:

Core Value #1:

Our Ceiling, *Their* Floor.

My husband and I are determined to make our victories--our ceiling--the starting place for our children, or their floor. For us, this means that we don't want our children to have to struggle and battle with the same things we have. From a *spiritual* perspective, this means teaching the children that they, too, can hear God. When something goes missing in our house-- for instance, a lost shoe--we have the children pray to ask God where it is. Then, we ask the kids to tell us if they saw something in their minds' eyes, or heard something in their hearts. If the kids get a picture of their room in their heads, then we begin the search for the shoe there. It is very frequent that, after praying, the kids are quickly able to claim their lost items. We use these moments to reinforce that God cares about all things, big and small, and also to teach the kids to learn how God speaks to them. As they continue to learn the ways in which God speaks to them, they will grow in confidence and faith, knowing that they hear God.

We also want our ceiling to be our children's floor in the area of *finances*, especially in the area of their college educations. My husband's family did not contribute to his college education. Since his parents were divorced, one parent wouldn't help, and the other couldn't help. , As a result, the responsibility of funding college fell solely on him. While attending community college, he was able to pay for his own schooling with his part-time job. However, once he transferred to university, he needed to take out student loans. Earning a master's degree in psychology has opened up amazing doors for him within his career, and there are no regrets. However, starting out a brand new career saddled with debt is a burden we would like to spare our children.

If we can help our children get through college without accruing student loan debt, it will free them up financially so that they are not beginning their careers, adult lives and marriages saddled with debt. This is not to say that any of our children will have a blank check when it comes to college. However, if they are working hard, are people of integrity, and have ambition attached to their dreams, we very much desire to invest in their futures and give them the gift of financial freedom.

To accomplish our mission of getting our kids through college or trade school debt free, we have taken on the whole "Rome-was-not-built-in-a-day" approach, and have set up mutual funds for each of our five children. Each month, a small amount of my husband's check gets automatically deposited into their accounts. As my husband continues to rise within his profession, and his paycheck increases, we will increase our monthly contributions, because any core value worth having is a core value worth investing in.

Core Value #2:

Leave It Better Than You Found It.

My husband and I believe that we are carriers of the Kingdom of God in our hearts. It is our desire that when people are around us, they encounter the Kingdom of God. This means that we should make people feel *safe* to be vulnerable, *encouraged* to dream big dreams, and *free* to walk in their destinies. As parents, our job is to instill these feelings of wellbeing and belonging in our children, and also to teach them to honor others in such a way that all of our lives create a domino effect of love, causing those who are around us to step into their destinies. When people come in contact with us, we want them to leave empowered, enriched and knowing their value.

Our *leave-it-better-than-you-found-it* core value also applies to places, including, but not limited to, public bathrooms. I remember when I was 32 weeks pregnant with my first son (40 weeks is full term). I was in a post office when, suddenly, my water broke. The sensation that I felt was similar to when I have had very heavy periods, so I felt like I needed to find a bathroom to figure out if I was bleeding or if my water had truly broken. I waddled next door to the Ace Hardware store, and somehow made it all the way back to the bathroom. In the bathroom, I confirmed that my water had indeed broken; and as I continued to leak fluid, every move I made became more difficult, since there was no longer the pillow of separation--the water--between me and our soon-to-be-son. Every move felt like bone on bone, and I was worried. He was not due for eight more weeks. As I was washing my hands in the bathroom, I noticed a few paper towels on the floor (probably someone's failed attempt at tossing them in the trash can). However they got there, I noticed them and thought to myself, *Normally, I would bend down and pick those up, but under the circumstances, I think I get a free pass.* The next thing I knew, I felt a stirring in my heart:

Is this who I am?

Someone who makes excuses when times get hard?

Is "leave it better than you found it" just a nice thing to say, or is it something that I truly believe and have adopted as a core value?

At that moment, I reached for the sink to balance myself, and I slowly lowered myself to reach and then throw away the towels. I waddled back to the front of the store, and then proceeded to drive myself to the hospital.

Two days later, our son was born. He was premature at 4 lbs., 5 oz., but he was breathing on his own.

We all have defining moments in our lives. In that public bathroom, with no audience to see my *good deeds*, and every excuse as to why I shouldn't live my values, I had one of those moments. It is these moments that allow us to see a true reflection of ourselves. In that moment, I chose to be a person of honor, rather than a victim of an unexpected preterm delivery. I chose to be the kind of person who lives my convictions, not just in public, but also in private places, too.

I believe that God strategically allowed me to have this core value moment as my body was preparing to give birth. As my body was transitioning, my heart was also being prepared for the enormous responsibility of stewarding our soon-to-be son. Would I be the best of who I was in both the private and public settings? Let's face it: most of our parenting is done in private. It's done in our homes, with doors and blinds closed, and it is there where our kids see the true us, without filters. I want my kids to know our family's core values, not because they are posted by the front door, but because they are written on our hearts, seen in our actions, and imparted to them daily.

Core Value #3:

Train Yourself Out of a Job.

In the competitive world that we live in, it is common for people to feel territorial about their positions, whether it is in the workplace, at church, or at home. It is the norm for people to be hesitant to allow others to help them. We often find self-worth and identity in the things we do, so the thought of someone else putting his or her stamp on one of our projects, or having to share the credit for a job well done, can be too much. Of course, we rarely admit this, even to ourselves. In fact, we will often complain that we have too much to do and that we wish someone would help; but when help is offered, we rarely accept. What excuse do we give for not accepting help? *They* would not do it right. It is not *their* responsibility. All the while, there is that nagging thought. *What if they do it better than me? What if I am no longer needed?*

The reality is that our hesitance to train ourselves out of a job is often the reason we get stuck in life. We don't get promoted because no one else can do our jobs. We become our own stumbling blocks. Within the family realm, this is seen in family recipes being lost forever because grandma never taught anyone else how to make it. We see it in teenagers who don't know how to do laundry, cook a meal, start the dishwasher or mow the lawn.

Our core value of training ourselves out of a job addresses two key heart issues:

1. By training ourselves out of a job, we tear down the lie that we are defined by what we do. We are not human doings, but human beings. When we allow others to step up into

their new seasons, it allows us to step into *our* new seasons.

2. When we train ourselves out of a job, we *empower* others.

Practicing the core value of training ourselves out of a job is actually an extremely liberating experience. It empowers others into a new purpose, while also making room for personal growth and change. Our identity becomes one of empowering others rather than one of being locked into a specific niche or role.

In this season of our own lives as parents, training ourselves out of a job looks like having the kids all do their own laundry, and assigning daily chores. For the younger ones, what this really means is working with them to put things away with a good attitude, and having them "help" us in our tasks. Knowing that children emulate what they see, rather than what they hear, it is important that our children "help" us maintain our home with the perspective that we all live here and we all deserve a nice place to live. In doing so, we are also instilling ownership and dignity.

Discussion Questions:

1. What core values act as a compass or theme song within your family?

2. In what ways can you make your ceiling your child(ren)'s floor?
3. What is something that you are doing as a parent right now that you are particularly proud of?

"May we shout for joy over your victory and lift up our banners in the name of our God. May the Lord grant all your requests."

- Psalms 20:5

"The plans of the diligent lead to profit as surely as haste leads to poverty."

- Proverbs 21:5

Dear God,

Give me wisdom as I raise my family. Teach me your ways so that I can impart them into my child(ren). Set the standard in me that you want my family to follow. Teach me to emulate you, and teach our family to reflect your love.

Amen.

Writing this particular book has been a dream of mine for over a decade. Now that this dream has turned into a reality, it is my prayer that as you made your way through these pages, you felt encouraged and empowered.

For those of you who, like me, look back on your childhood with fondness, I am sure that you could relate to many of my stories. I pray that my memories act as a catalyst to reignite some of your most treasured moments, and that you have been inspired to continue to build on the foundation that you were given.

For those of you who could relate more to my parents--having a childhood without the essential elements, or even worse, a childhood filled with abuse and/or neglect--I pray that this book brought you hope. I pray that you feel empowered knowing that with God, all things are possible. My mom and dad, despite their own wounds and holes from childhood, were amazing parents; and no matter what season of life you are in, you, too, can find your way.

There is no such thing as a perfect person or perfect parent. As great as my parents were, they were not perfect. They had their moments of failure. If you asked them, I am sure that they could tell you of countless ways in which they missed their desired target, but those failures have not defined them. They have not camped in or embraced their failures, but have chosen to grow as individuals and as a couple. Sure, there were times when tempers were lost, words were said, and mistakes were made, but it was not these moments that defined them or me. In life, all of us eventually come to a place where we have to evaluate our prominent memories, our past and current actions, and our core beliefs, to determine how these will define our lives.

My parents were not perfect. I am not perfect. You are not perfect. There is, however, a perfect God in heaven, a loving and kind Father who brings healing to the brokenhearted, forgives our mistakes, and desires mercy over judgement every time.

Blessings to you and your family.

About the Author

Joy Adams is married to Bruce Adams III, her best friend and husband for over nineteen years. Together, Joy and Bruce are the parents to five children, two naturally born, and three born from the heart. As a third generation teacher, Joy taught high school for nine years and loved it. In 2014, she was privileged to be promoted to her ultimate dream job as a stay-at-home mom.

Joy Adams is passionate about sharing her faith in God, nurturing healthy families, and promoting community, both locally and globally. You can read more from Joy Adams on her blog, www.inspirationofjoy.com. There, she shares experiences from her everyday life in hope that they will inspire others to live their faith, find joy in the mundane, and connect within their communities.

What My Parents Did Right is Joy Adams's first published work.

Joy Adams would love to hear from you. You can contact her through her website, www.inspirationofjoy.com, or by emailing joyadamsblog@gmail.com. Joy is available for limited speaking engagements. You can find her itinerary on her website.

Recommended Reading

Teach them to Fly by Laura Mailhot is a valuable resource filled with practical tools that really work. I know this with absolute certainty because I myself was "taught to fly". As the youngest daughter to Laura Mailhot, I experienced firsthand the effectiveness of her methods. *Teach them to Fly* effectively blends the clear parameters of classical parenting while also taking into account the individual child's needs, interests, and personality. The methods laid out in this book are simple, straightforward and timeless.